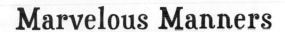

Marvelous Manners

Cowboys Can Be Kind

Timothy Knapman

Illustrated by **Jimothy Oliver**

QEB Publishing

Cowboys should be **brave** and **true**,
for that is the cowboy way.

But Cowboy Jack was **not** like that. . .
. . .until one special day.

Way out West in the playground,
Jack rode his cowboy bike.

He said, "I'll go wherever **I want**, and I'll pedal as fast as **I like!**"

He **didn't care** about honest folk,
who played like **good** girls and boys.

Without warning, he'd **shoot** right past them—
and **scatter** their games and toys!

He took people's things without asking
and shouted, "**You can't catch me!**"

He **laughed** when he let go of Lily's balloon,
and it got stuck in a tree.

Then the day came when Jack saw a puddle next to Eve in her **brand-new dress**.

And he thought, **"I'd love to splash her!"**
And then—well, can you guess?

Jack was pedaling toward **that puddle**
when, just a few feet ahead. . .

...a **naughty** boy went cycling by,
and he splashed Jack **instead!**

Eve pointed at Jack, who was **dirty** and **wet**, and she gave him a piece of her mind.

"It **serves** you perfectly right," she said,
"for being so very **unkind!**"

"I never knew that it **felt** this **bad**," said Jack.
"I was **just** having fun!"

So he went up to everyone saying **sorry**
for all the **mean things** he'd done.

From then on, Jack was **different**
and did what a cowboy should.

He was **friendly** and joined in the games—
he was **kind** and **helpful** and **good**.

In no time at all, he had plenty of **friends**-
he couldn't stop **smiling** all day.

There were races to run and swings to be swung
and so many **fun games** to **play!**

If you're ever way out West in the playground
and see Jack, I think that you'll find,
he's a cowboy who's **brave** and **true**—
he's a **cowboy who can be kind!**

Next Steps

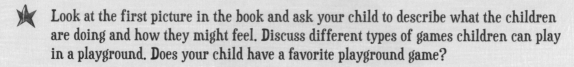

⭐ Look at the first picture in the book and ask your child to describe what the children are doing and how they might feel. Discuss different types of games children can play in a playground. Does your child have a favorite playground game?

⭐ Ask your child what they know about cowboys—for example, where they live, what they look like, and what they wear.

⭐ Talk about Jack's naughty behavior and its effect on other children and on Jack himself.

⭐ Discuss the moment that makes Jack change the way he treats others. Why does he decide to change? Does he feel sorry for other children now that he understands how bad he made them feel?

⭐ Ask your child to give examples of unkind behavior and examples of friendly behavior. What different consequences do these behaviors have? You could even use role play to show the difference between unfriendly and friendly ways of behaving.

⭐ Explain that selfish, unkind, and bad behavior will drive away other children, which might make your child feel lonely. Talk about the fact that being kind and considerate makes it more fun to play with others and easier to make friends. Also mention that even a strong and brave child can be kind and friendly and say sorry.

⭐ Emphasize that the way children behave toward others can affect the way they feel. It also affects how other people treat them, and whether others like them or not.

Consultant: Cecilia A. Essau
Editor: Alexandra Koken
Designer: Andrew Crowson

Copyright © QEB Publishing 2012

First published in the United States by
QEB Publishing, Inc.
3 Wrigley, Suite A
Irvine, CA 92618

www.qed-publishing.co.uk

ISBN 978 1 60992 344 0

Printed in China

Library of Congress Cataloging-in-Publication Data

Knapman, Timothy.
Cowboys can be kind / by Timothy Knapman ; illustrated by Jimothy Rovolio.
     p. cm. -- (Marvelous manners)
  Summary: Cowboy Jack has learned the hard way the importance of being unselfish and kind.
  ISBN 978-1-60992-269-6 (hardcover, library bound)
  [1. Stories in rhyme. 2. Selfishness--Fiction. 3. Kindness--Fiction.] I. Rovolio, Jimothy, ill. II. Title.
  PZ8.3.K73Cow 2013
  [E]--dc23

                                          2011051891